15 DAYS OF HELL
One man's battle for Peleliu

DR. JORDAN WINER
AND
LEW SHUMAN

15 DAYS
OF
HELL

Copyright © 2014
Lewis A. Shuman
ISBN-13: 978-1511976374
ISBN-10: 1511976373
Library of Congress Control Number:
LCCN: 2015907044
Publisher:
CreateSpace Independent Publishing Platform
Printed in North Charleston, South Carolina

"I hit the beach with 40 Corpsman after one day
18 were left"
Chief Pharmacist Mate Morris Estes, *Action at
Anguar, Palau 1945 World War II Pacific Film*

+

"You will take no prisoners, you will kill every
yellow son-of-a-bitch, and that's it."
Marine Colonel "Chesty" Puller

Dedicated
To all the Docs that served and saved.

Contents:

Foreword

During World War II our fathers and our grandfathers willingly enlisted in huge numbers in all branches of the military. People of all races, religions and sexes went off to war in support of the principles of democracy. Millions wore the uniforms and thousands paid the ultimate sacrifice. They served proudly and honorably in World War II.

After his passing in 1997, Jordan Winer's family discovered a diary. They did not know that this journal even existed. His son-in-law and family decided to share with you his personal moments as a young navy man serving his country thousands of miles away from home.

Jordan Winer enlisted and was trained to be a Pharmacist Mate/ Corpsman. His unit was the famed 1st Marine Division and he participated in their attack of the island of Peleliu during the battle that became known as the "Battle of Bloody Nose Ridge" in September of 1944.

"Doc" Winer's personal diary relives his fifteen days on the sun-backed South Pacific atoll called Peleliu. The island was the stronghold for an estimated 11,000 fanatical fighters of the Emperor's Imperial 14th Division. Through his personal first-hand account, you will witness the compassion, the tenacity and the courage of the participants on both sides. In the end, the victory cost the marines dearly with over 1,200 dead and over 5,000 wounded or missing.

Sadly, for the enemy garrison defending on Peleliu it turned out to be a no-win situation. Of the 11,000 Japanese soldiers at the beginning of the fight only about 300 survived.

This text will be an inspiration to all that hold dear what our parents' generation contributed to winning the war and making our country great.

Dan Simmons
Corpsman U.S. Navy and Vietnam Veteran
St Louis, Missouri

Prologue:

Jordan Winer was 23 years old when he joined up to fight in World War II. Originally from Salem, Massachusetts, Jordan and his younger brother Stanley both answered our nation's call. Stanley went into the Coast Guard while older brother Jordan joined the Navy. His job in the service was that of a pharmacist mate.

After his basic training and advanced schooling at Norfolk, Virginia, he was assigned to the United States Marines where he received a promotion to Pharmacist Mate First-Class. His unit was Mobile Hospital 9 and MOB-9 and he was attached to the 1st Battalion, 1st Regiment 1st Marine Division.

"Doc's" theater of operation was a chain of islands called the Palau Islands. They were well over 8,666 miles from his Salem, Massachusetts home. Jordan Winer's contribution to the war took place during a two-week period in 1944 on the small South Pacific Palau Nation Island called Peleliu.

The well-defended island of Peleliu was invaded by the United States Marine Corps and Army during September of 1944. It was a heavily fortified Japanese held atoll with 11,000 well-fortified and battle-hardened fanatical fighters of the 14th Imperial Japanese Division. The deeply dug-in cave dwelling Japanese anxiously lay in wait for the Americans.

The ensuing fight eventually became known historically as "The Battle of Bloody Nose Ridge." In time the bloody encounter between the United States and Japan was proven to be a terrible waste of American and Japanese lives.

The assault was a folly of tremendous proportion. The original battle plan established by General MacArthur called for the taking of the island and its airfield. The airport would be used as a stepping stone for our air forces to launch strikes on the Japanese homeland. The capturing of the island would cost the marines an estimated 1,200 marines killed and another 5,000 wounded or missing. The 1st Marine Division was decimated with a 71% casualty rate.

On the opposing side, out of the 11,000 defending members of the emperor's Japanese 14th Infantry Division there were only 300 survivors capable of walking out of their jungle strongholds. The Emperor's 14th Division ceased to exist as a cohesive fighting force.

The American's faced a determined enemy that stubbornly held on if they could.

Japanese resistance continued on the island after the battle was won. It officially ended three and a half years later when Lieutenant Ei Yamaguchi and 33 soldiers emerged on Peleliu in late March of 1947 after attacking the U.S. Marine Corps detachment stationed on the island. Only after reinforcements were sent in, along with a Japanese admiral who could convince them that their war was over; they walked out of the cave they were defending and finally surrendered in April 1947. [1]

Lt. Ei Yamaguchi

Public Domain

Yamaguchi, appearing on the NBC Dateline program *"Return to Peleliu"* in August of 1995 was asked: "What were the orders of the Japanese troops; didn't you know the war was over?"

Yamaguchi replied: "We couldn't believe that we had lost. We were always instructed that we could never lose. It is the Japanese tradition that we must fight until we die, until the end."

Now almost 70 years after the battle, it was reported in *Japan Today*, that *The Australian Broadcasting Company* in anticipation of a visit to Peleliu by the current Emperor Akihito and his wife the Empress Michiko *The Australian Broadcasting Company* commissioned a search of caves that had been sealed up ever since the end of the war due to the un-exploded armaments and ammunition that was in them.

Upon entry of what was described as a "One thousand man cave" searchers discovered the skeletal remains of what appeared to be six Japanese soldiers. They were six of an estimated 2,600 soldiers that have never been accounted for.

The remains that were discovered would be sent home for proper burial and a commitment that other sealed caves would be re-opened and inspected. Any additional remains found would be repatriated and returned to Japan.

A Thousand Man Cave

Courtesy: Australian Broadcasting Co. and Japan Today

More information about Dr. Jordan Winer and his service to our country.

After a long career in podiatric medicine; serving the people of Chelsea, Massachusetts, "Doc" Winer passed away on May 13, 1997. His family discovered in his personal items a diary. No one knew of its prior existence. This single-spaced typed war diary was compiled by Jordan while he was a U. S. Navy corpsman.

It was his first-person account of the battle for Peleliu. Several years after the war ended, then Dr. Jordan Winer was informed by the Navy Department that he had been cited for bravery under fire. For his action and participation, he was awarded the Bronze Star. This award was in addition to the Purple Heart he earned for wounds received in battle.

This diary is "Doc" Winer's personal fifteen days of hell while performing his duties above and beyond while administering aid and comfort to his marines. You will read his frank, honest and un-edited words and with him, you will feel the scorching heat, stifling humidity and never ending bloody fighting along with the fear, compassion, courage and keen insight that was observed by "Doc" Winer on Peleliu.

This memoir is his testimony. It was his personal witness of his fifteen days in hell.

Chapter 1

"Yes we'll rally round the flag boys; we'll rally once again, shouting the battle cry of freedom."[2] *The Battle Cry of Freedom* was written in 1862 by George Root was intended as a motivator to encourage enlistments in the Civil War.

Fifty years after the Civil War on the eve of World War I, the troops were the recipient of the works of George M. Cohan and his fervent, patriotic *Over There*. We told the world that, "the Yanks are coming…and we won't be back till it's over, over there."

During World War I in America it was a deceivingly different time. While most people supported our Country's involvement in Europe; many others preferred that the United States would have not been involved or included in what became "The Great War." There was fierce resentment of Mr. Wilson's desire to police the world.

Unlike World War I, it was different for World War II. Americans rallied around the flag especially after the shock of December 7, 1941 and the Japanese sneak attacks on our Pacific Fleet anchored at Pearl Harbor as well as, Hickam Field and Schofield Barracks.

The soldiers, sailors and airman of the "rising sun" also simultaneously attacked and occupied Wake Island, Guam, and the Republic of the Philippines along with the British Crown colony of Hong Kong. These hostilities against the United States unleashed a mighty and unequalled storm of manpower and western industrial might that led to a massive marshaling of men and machines on two fronts; Fortress Europe and the Pacific.

It was World War II songs like *Boogie Woogie Bugle Boy* by The Andrews Sisters and *Der Fuehrer's Face* by Spike Jones provided inspirational entertainment and humor to our troops and the folks at home during our country's time of war.

First VE or Victory in Europe came on May 8, 1945. The Third Reich's reign of terror was over. Hitler was dead from a well-placed bullet to the brain and the allies turned their power and might toward the east and the "Rising Sun."

Great strides had been made in the Pacific. Island hoping by the allies especially the United States Marines were having a positive impact. General Douglas MacArthur had succeeded in returning to the Philippines. One island-by-one the Japanese were slowly being driven back. The tide was turning on the Japanese. But it was to be at an amazing cost to the Japanese people.

The stubborn Japanese resisted surrender. Plans were on the drawing board for an American invasion of the Japanese homeland. Allied casualties would be atrocious.

Before the planned invasion could be launched, it took two atomic bombs; one dropped on the city of Hiroshima on August 6, 1945 and another three days later on August 9, 1945 obliterating the cities of Hiroshima and Nagasaki. Only then did the government of Japan and its people realize that any more resistance would be futile.

Similarly, the West did not want to risk the predicted deaths of thousands of military personnel if the United States was forced into an invasion of the Japanese homeland.

The bombings of Hiroshima and Nagasaki killed an estimated 240,000 men, women and children. The United States had unleashed the power of the atom with devastating effects on the people of Japan. After the pounding of Hiroshima and Nagasaki, the Japanese finally had enough.

On August 15, 1945, Emperor Hirohito spoke directly to his people. His speech would be the first time the Emperor of Japan's voice would be heard publically. Many Nipponese in the general population thought of his imperial majesty as a "god-like" being that was above mortal man.

The Emperor spoke to his subjects:

"To our good and loyal subjects: After pondering deeply the general trends of the world and the actual conditions obtaining in our empire today, we have decided to affect a settlement of the present situation by resorting to an extraordinary measure.

" We have ordered our Government to communicate to the Governments of the United States, Great Britain, China and the Soviet Union that our empire accepts the provisions of their joint declaration."

Emperor Hirohito

On September 2, 1945 aboard the battleship USS Missouri anchored in Tokyo Bay, General Douglas MacArthur accompanied by members of the allied nations presented to the assembled Japanese the terms of surrender and capitulation. MacArthur accepted the signature of the Japanese delegation.

General MacArthur on the USS Missouri addressed the Japanese entourage on the terms of surrender.

In a bit of showmanship, the General deliberately positioned officers and sailors around him all of whom were in excess six feet in height to dwarf and humiliate the Japanese signatories as they made the slow painful walk across the deck to accept the terms of capitulation and their admission of defeat.

Japanese delegation accepting the terms of surrender on the USS Missouri

Courtesy: Naval Historical Command

Finally, in September of 1945 America would be at peace.

Chapter 2

Growing up in the Dorchester section of Boston, Massachusetts during the 1950's and early 1960's the war to me and my friends was displayed every Saturday afternoon at the neighborhood theaters on Blue Hill Avenue. We spent our quarters to attend the Morton, Oriental and Franklin Park Theaters. I fondly remember in addition to the feature films we watched spellbound as the news reels with Lowell Thomas preceded the feature presentation with news from around the world.

In black and white on the big screen we were witness to events that were taking place all over the world. For my twenty-five cents, we were captivated by the news reels and the feature films that would follow. There on the big screen was Burt Lancaster and Montgomery Clift in *From Here to Eternity*, Richard Widmark in *The Halls of Montezuma*, William Bendix in *Guadalcanal Diary*, and later Steve McQueen in *The Great Escape* and Otto Preminger's *The Longest Day*.

That was my entertainment growing up in the city. War was glorified! John Wayne always portrayed the good guy. In hindsight, the films were a celluloid passion play of good over evil and the enemy was portrayed in stereotypical fashion be they German or Japanese.

To us our movie perception of the Japanese was that of a buck-toothed little man with bad eyes. They desired to kill us all in "Banzai" charges like in *Guadalcanal Diary* and then there was the German Hun, depicted by Marlon Brando in the film *The Young Lions* portraying a large grotesque Jew-hating character that threatened our way of life.

As a young child, I remember walking down the street with my mother and one day at the cobbler's store on the corner of Calendar Street and Blue Hill Avenue I asked her, "Mama, why does the man have a number on his arm? As we were walking out she replied, "He was held prisoner by some very bad people."

Later I learned exactly what she meant! Our neighborhood cobbler was a survivor of the concentration camps that filled Nazi Germany with the victims of Hitler's "Final Solution."   In my neighborhood, there were quite a few people who had survived German cruelty with a tattoo on their forearm as a life-long reminder of their suffering at the hands of a nation gone mad.

America during World War II was fighting a war on many fronts. In Europe and the East, it was the Western allies and Stalin's Russia against Germany's Third Reich.

Battles raged in Europe and Africa and to the west in the Pacific against the Imperial Empire of Japan.   World War II was a global war.

It was under these rumbles of war and attacks that our fathers, cousins and uncles answered the call to serve. They lined up at recruiting offices all over America. Whites, Blacks, Jews and Gentiles all raised their right hands and swore to defend America and its Constitution…their goal was to end the tyranny that wanted to enslave the free-world.

After the war ended our fathers, uncles and grand fathers were welcomed home by a grateful nation and pursued their lives where they had left off. They performed their military duties proudly and when they came home they were reluctant to talk about their experiences. Working, marrying, raising a family and pursuing the American Dream was their goal. I don't remember my dad talking about his war-time experience. It was only after a little prodding would he open on what he did in the war.

I knew he had been a medic in the Army Air Corps and had spent his entire military career at various posts stateside. He was stationed at Fort Polk administering to servicemen that had contracted Leprosy and other tropical maladies. His specialty at Twenty-Nine Palms in the Mojave Desert was treating heat-stroke. When he returned to Boston he married Selma Openhiem and they had one child; yours truly.

He was a member of the Jewish War Veterans Post 630 and once or twice a year he would put on his service cap and help in collecting money for their charities. It became a regular site to see these veterans out on street corners selling their peanuts to raise monies to be used to help other less-privileged veterans.

While watching television together my dad would occasionally respond to us when we would mention a certain actress on the small screen he'd pipe in with "I danced with her." He then reminded us that he had spent an occasional weekend on pass with his buddies in Los Angeles.

Each visit included a stop at the Hollywood Canteen. Admission to the Canteen was free if the serviceman was in uniform. During the War, the Canteen was manned every day by the actors and actresses of Hollywood. Hundreds of well-known entertainers willingly donated their time and provided a smile, served refreshments, offered an occasional dance and some friendly conversation for the guys who were far from home.

Jordan Winer, my late father-in law was a veteran of the United States Navy. While we knew, he had served we had no idea where or what he had been through. Most veterans rarely talked about their war experiences.

As mentioned, they quietly and un-ceremoniously returned to the homes that they left behind and picked up where their every-day lives began before the war. It was not until after his death in 1997 that we discoverd his personal war diary. For over fifty-four years it lay untouched and un-read.

Chapter 3

By September of 1944, the war in Europe was continuing with break outs favoring the allies. Fortress Europe had been invaded three months earlier in June on the Normandy Peninsula and the Army was making tremendous strides in its march toward Berlin. American combat losses in Europe were totaling close to 180,000 killed and the expected losses in the Pacific would be horrific; especially with the anticipated invasion of the Japanese homeland by allied forces.

The war in the Pacific was continuing and was nowhere near its end. Allied advances were significant but still the toll in lives was continuing to grow. Island hoping to the west had begun to eliminate Japanese footholds and for the advancing forces there seemed to be a "light at the end of the tunnel." The marines had the grimy task of pushing the Japanese off these islands. Slowly, Americans became familiar with names like Wake, Midway, Guadalcanal, and Peleiu then Iwo Jima and Okinawa.

Later the islands of Iwo Jima and Okinawa would be bloody stepping stones for the marines. Before the taking of Okinawa and the flag rising at Suribachi on Iwo Jima there was one more stop for marines along the way. Peleliu was part of the island nation of Palau. The tiny atoll was located 2,000 miles south of Japan and over 6,000 miles from the United States it was considered a vital stop for marines in the battle for control of the Pacific. It had an airfield that at the time was deemed mission essential in order for the allies to bring the war closer to the Japanese homeland. So, in September of 1944, the stage was set for the battle for Peleiu.

Marine Major General William Rupertus commander of 1st Division—predicted the island would be secured "within four days."[3]

However, the battle lasted over two months and it had the highest casualty rate of any battle in the Pacific War.[4]

In hindsight, it would be the bloodiest and bitterest battle of the war fought by the Marines in the Pacific theater.[5]

The first obstacle faced by the marines upon landing was the land itself. The terrain appeared to be "a complex system of sharply uplifted coral ridges, knobs, valleys, and sinkholes…and (it) provided excellent emplacements for cave and tunnel defenses."

Secondly, the Japanese had the luxury of time on their side. With the aide of conscripted non-Japanese slave laborers; the captured Chinese and Koreans working for the Japanese constructed vast underground defensive positions that were practicably in- penetrable to bombing and artillery. By the time the marines landed, the Japanese were dug in and secure in their defensive positions eagerly awaiting the arrival of the marines. What was "a walk in the park" by some American officers would end up as a bloodletting for both sides.

The Japanese had made the most of what this terrain provided during their extensive period of occupation and defensive preparations.[6]

Colonel Kunio Nakagawa

The second impediment facing the Marines was the defense of the island by the Japanese.

"Colonel Kunio Nakagawa was the officer who was to command the force on Peleliu, He was supported by his superior, Lieutenant General Sadae Inoue back on the Island of Koror.

The Japanese concept of defense had changed. Instead of relying upon a presumed moral superiority to defeat the attackers at the beach, and then to use their bushido spirit and banzai tactics to throw any survivors back into the sea, Peleliu's defenders would delay the attacking Marines if they could, attempt to bleed them as heavily as possible.

Rather than depending upon spiritual superiority, they would combine the devilish terrain with the stubborn, disciplined, Japanese soldiers to relinquish Peleliu at the highest cost to the invaders.

This unpleasant surprise for the marines marked a new and important adjustment to the Japanese tactics which were employed earlier in the war."[7]

It is my intent to take you back to 1944 through the eyes of one of the battle's participants, Jordan Winer. What you will read will be unedited, raw human emotion from a twenty-five-year-old describing the hardships, losses, craziness and successes gained by our fighting men in the Pacific. Punctuation, spelling and context will be untouched and left as originally written.

His diary began on September 15, 1944 while still, aboard his transport ship waiting to disembark. "Doc" Winer's words will be italicized.

Day 1-September 15, 1944

"D" day was to be the fifteenth of September, 1944. Aboard the USS Warren, there was little confusion, but rather on the eve of the "blitz" everyone was in good spirits. Reveille was held at two-thirty A.M. and [sic] all hands enjoyed a light but hearty breakfast of bacon and eggs. We "put our gear on" soon after and waited the word to lower away into the Higgins boats.

It was now approximately five o'clock and we were riding the waters in circles all the boats in our wave waiting their turn to go to the line of departure.

Our wave was scheduled to go in at "H" plus seventy as we circled around, we saw the shelling from the huge 14 inch guns of the nearby Mississippi.

The Naval [sic] gunfire and shelling had been going on for over a week and now it was even more intense. There were hundreds of planes circling overhead which lent a feeling of security to us as we watched them go in and bomb and strafe the island of Pelelieu. We had to laugh as we envisioned our foe taking this devastating fire and bombing. We could never for a moment doubt that it was taking a terrific toll of the enemy. But we were very wrong in our reasoning.

"H" hour had passed and it was 0930 as we reached the line of departure. We weren't certain, but we thought as we were going in, that we saw enemy mortar or artillery fire falling in the water up ahead. We changed from the Higgins boats into the LCVP's without incident and now, we were positive the fire we thought had existed was an actuality.

The enemy was dropping mortars all over the beach with great accuracy and we ducked down plenty low in our "Amph-track.[sic]" Above the din of the engine, we could we could hear firing and glancing up, I observed several Amph-tracts [sic] that had been hit and were burning

We were landed somewhat to the right of our designated spot and found ourselves knee-deep in water as we disembarked. The mortars were raising hell with everything in sight as we made a run for the beach and the shelter of a coral cliff.

We no sooner reached this point, the call arose for corpsman, and Drouin, Beal, Hatterer, Dr. Hagerty and I took off for the area from whence the call came. Here, we found at least twenty men badly wounded and an estimated ten dead. This included two corpsman as we soon found out.

The outfit was "K" Co. 3rd Bn 1st Marines and they had been mortared mercilessly. The mortar fragments were flying everywhere and Drouin caught a piece on his back and I a fragment on my hand.

We went to work patching the wounded up as best we could and placed them on waiting amphtracts [sic] for immediate evacuation.

Department of Defense Photo (USN) 283745

In reality, "As seen from the air on D-Day, 15 September 1944 "K" Company, 3rd Battalion, 1st Marines "was on the extreme left flank of the entire 1st Division."[8]

Company K of the 1st Marines' 3rd Battalion, commanded by Capt. George P. Hunt, had the mission of capturing the Point and subduing Japanese crossfire. Of the 235 men Hunt led against the Point, more than two-thirds were killed or wounded taking the position."[9]

A call soon arose from over the cliff for a corpsman, and I ran up forty five in my hand. I saw my first dead nip here and his body was lying in front of a cave, which was of thick concrete. At this point, the front lines were between twenty five and fifty yards ahead and the man I was called to attend was beyond all stage of medical assistance. I felt doubtful that the cave-like concrete installation that I described above was empty for some unknown reason, perhaps instinct, but I volunteered the services of a couple of rifle-men and we started in.

We took exactly one step when a hand grenade came flying out and hit the fellow on the right of me on the chin and glanced off my left elbow, the fellow on my left hastily picked it up and threw it away. We ducked behind a blind spot in the opening of the cave and as we did so, the grenade exploded as simultaneously, rifle fire came from the interior of the cave. If the fire had preceded the throwing of the grenade all might have been over for this little boy and my diary would have ended at this point. (Close Call #1)

It was now approximately 1130 and I ran to the beach and commandeered a squad of demolition men who blew up this beach installation. I later found out that there were six nippos [sic] found inside.

I then made my way to Beach White Two and we commenced to set up our aid station. There was little or no cover here and I realize later that had the Japs boxed their mortar fire here on the beach, we wouldn't have had a chance.

(I knew now that the big joke we had enjoyed in the boats about the island being wiped out by ship and plane fire was a joke alright, only it was on us).

While meditating, a cry for corpsman again rang out and this time, Marsino and I took off in the direction of the call as the rest of the boys worked frantically to dig themselves [sic] in. Mars and I ran to our left and inland approximately seventy five yards, but couldn't find any wounded man there. We sat on a log to rest and as we drank from our canteens, a sniper started to take pot shots at us. We lit out for the beach Marsino in the lead and I shouted to him to run in a zig zag manner and we hit the beach in nothing flat.

No sooner had I sat down on the beach when Jackson of the Q.M. corps called "Winer" and pointed to where a man had been hit a few yards to the left. There was a sniper nearby and everyone ducked low in their fox-holes.

I ran over and patched him up and tagged him, he wasn't hurt badly but was angry to think that he had been hit. I tagged him and was starting back when I felt a rifle prodding me in the butt, turning I looked directly into the intensely determined face of a negro, who said, "Is yo'all [sic] a corpsman?"

All he said when I answered affirmatively was, "Follow me." I Did. He led me to an amphtract [sic] that was still smoldering and inside was his buddy. I climbed in and examined him, but he was no more.

Back at the Bn. aid [sic] station I hurried pausing long enough to pick up some salmon and beans which was conveniently lying on the beach from an overturned jeep trailer. By now, the casualties were being carried in by stretcher and we were busy for the next few hours treating them and tagging them and seeing that they were evacuated safely to the ships.

We were setting up plasma units and suspending the bottles from rifles which we stuck in the sand. A most convenient and effective method of administration.

The stretcher bearers performed their jobs well and it might be well to mention the excellent way they worked throughout the operation. Our patients were evacuated almost immediately after treatments and our evacuations were consistently speedy throughout the operation.

At this stage, we were so close to the beach that the patients could be carried by stretcher bearers, later however the evacuations were effected by amphtracts [sic] and ambulances.

Fletcher HA1 was commencing to get ill at this stage and Lovitz another of my men was also feeling a bit shaky. For the most part, however the men were all right. Dr. Hagerty kept up our moral by his good humor. It was now commencing to get dark, this day had practically flown and I put to good use the chow I had confiscated from the jeep trailer.

Our 1st Battalion had been originally scheduled to go into attack at a point known as O3, but had been on assault from the moment we had landed. "A" Co. our reserve company had been moved into the front lines to fill in a gap. "Was this to be another Tarawa?" It certainly appeared that way judging from the casualties and the slow progress we were making. Every inch of ground gained was taking it's [sic] cost in lives and blood. I hadn't had a chance to dig a fox-hole and although Dr. Schoff offered to share his with me, I declined in favor of a spot behind a tree that had once been thriving with coconuts, but was now a mere stump.

Everyone else was dug in as we settled down for the first night. Drouin was sacked in with Lovitz who was acting up strongly he kept repeating, we're done we're finished, let me out etc. and Drouin had all he could to do to restrain him.

Except for the land crabs, the flares and sporadic firing, I actually slept a few hours and awoke somewhat refreshed.

I was saddened somewhat by the news that one of my men, Auerbach had been killed by a sniper upon landing in performance of his duty for he was running after Lt. Mueller of "C" co. who had been hit when Auerbach got it. From A Co. we learned that Sr. Corpsman LePage and PhN3/c Bingham had been wounded and evacuated.

Chapter 4

Day 2-September 16, 1944

The second day dawned clear and warm. We had no sooner completed eating our morning rations when the casualties commenced to arrive. They were rolling in all day and we worked madly and cooperated nicely. We were clicking very well and handling our patient expertly.

A Fox-Movietone photographer snapped my picture as I was administering plasma to a patient. He later told me that this was the worst blitz he had ever made, and he was a veteran of Africa, Guam, Saipan, Gloucester and Tarawa. I said "Worse than Tarawa?" Hell yes was his answer. We learned that morning the "A" Co. on our left flank had held the Jay-boys at bay all night despite many of their famed banzai counter attacks.

An interesting side story evolved: "Doc" Winer's Brother Stanley a coast guardsman was stationed half way around the world in Norfolk, Virginia while his brother was grinding it out in Peleliu. While on Liberty he was attending a movie theater in Norfolk in December of 1944.

Stanley had last seen his brother Jordan in 1943 while both were stationed in Norfolk. The Movietone News Reel was about the battle for the Island of Peleliu, suddenly he realized he was watching his brother administering plasma to a wounded marine.

He jumped up and yelled, "That's my brother, that's my brother." The theater manager and projectionist stopped the film, brought up the house lights and cut out a couple of frames of the news reel and gave them to Stanley.

Actual Photograph of "Doc" Winer captured by Fox Movietone Photographer. Courtesy: Winer Family, Fox and National World War II Museum

Newspaper article about brother seeing brother on Movietone Newsreel

Courtesy: Salem Evening News December 1944

Transcript from Salem Evening News

Movies Reveal Brother's War Work, Location

Pharmacist's Mate First Class, Jordan Joseph Winer, 24, of 22A Hazel Street has been serving with a Marine Division in the Pacific area for the past 15 months., but his exact whereabouts was not known until a little more than a week ago when his brother Stanley, a seaman first class in the Coast Guard saw his brother giving blood plasma to a wounded comrade on Peleliu Island on the approaches to the Philippines in a newsreel in a theater in Norfolk, VA. The newsreel is now being shown at the Salem Paramount Theater.

The action shots showed the First marine division in operations against the Nippons. Then in full view Jordan was shown performing the duties of a pharmacist-the unsung hero of the war. Stanley leaped to his feet as he saw his brother in the newsreel. The manager snipped off a few feet of the news reel showing the Salem boy and presented it to Stanley, now home on leave.

Jordan first served at the U. S. Naval Hospital in Brisbane, Australia, before moving out to the various Pacific Islands as they were conquered one by one from the Japanese. While in Brisbane, he was contributing editor to the "Mobster," publication of a mobile naval hospital. Many of his poems have been published in the "Mobster."

Stanley has been in the Coast Guard for two years and is on duty out of Norfolk. He last saw his brother in Norfolk in April, 1943."

"C" Company had also been busy and had driven off an eight jap [sic] tank attack aided by a couple of General Shermans [sic] and a bazooka. The two that tried to escape were hit by rocket guns fired from the planes.

O'Toole HA1c came in from the B Company lines looking rather shaky and spent and I made him spend the rest of the day and the night with us. Fletcher HA1c had to be evacuated as ill though I think he could have stuck it out. I'll reserve my opinion of him. We kept busy treating all the casualties as they came in and at 1500, we got the word to move on up the lines. A good sign, but judging by the number of wounded, and from all reports, we weren't doing any winning.

We set up our B.A.S (Battalion Aid Station) at a spot directly in front of a Jap anti-tank trap. It was here that we were supposed to have been within an hour after landing on D day.

The area in which we were now located was literally covered with decaying Japanese and marine dead. They gave off a terrible stench and they could have only been there for two days. The nips turned jet black when they died and maggots were already running all over them.

We learned that "Chicken" Oldham, HA1c had been killed that day in gallant performance of his duty with "A" Company. We hadn't heard from any of our company corpsman and as night was settling in, we were commencing to feel somewhat concerned over them.

We made cocoa, ate C rations and Levy from N. Y. a stretcher bearer assigned to us settled down with me to spend the night. We slept on a stretcher in a shell crater. Sporadic firing continued all during the night, and both our own and hostile flares kept the skies brightly illuminated.

These flares caused the tree branches to throw off grotesque shadows and figures, but despite all this, I slept soundly.

Chapter 5

Day 3-September 17, 1944

The morning of the seventeenth dawned bright and rather hot. Just how hot I had no idea. I detailed Beal PhM2C to set up a shelter for the wounded and he and some men from "E" Medical Co. constructed a crude but none the less excellent shelter. The casualties for the morning were rather light Thank God for that. At about ten a.m. we were given the word to move out. We packed our gear on stretchers and set out on a hot march for about a half mile til we came to a tremendous Jap block-house. Fully 50 yards long and 20 yards wide. It was of concrete and steel about two and a half feet thick and only the 14 inch guns of a battleship had made an impression on its side. Nothing else could have penetrated this impregnable fortress. I glanced inside, and the stench stifled me.

There were 4 dead Jap bodies inside and four gaping holes in the sides of the walls where the fourteen inch shells from the Navy guns had penetrated. Shore to ship communications had been no doubt instrumental in knocking out this installation. Dead Jap and marine bodies were to be seen all around the area.

Inside this blockhouse were many mines and booby traps left by the enemy prior to their retreating. We didn't dare enter until demolitions men had first rid the place of this menace. Outside and to the left of the road were to be seen what was to have been the start of two more of these block houses. Evidence of concrete, cement mixer and sand were there. There were many pamphlets, souvenirs, pictures etc. in the blockhouse and intelligence received most of these.

Nearby was a Jap Officer's Quarters and Quartermaster storehouse and here the boys had a field day picking out Jap clothes. We set up our aid station in front of the blockhouse and outside we were striving to build a shelter form the hot sun and treat the wounded that were already coming in at the same time.

Pattee, a friend from the Comm section was among the first of the casualties. What a picture he made as he walked down the road as casually as if he were strolling to church only his arm or what had once been his arm was dangling in an unorthodox angle and was being held I observed by only a strand of tendon and skin. Dr. Hagerty completed the amputation and with a well applied battle dressing and after administrating him 500c.c. off blood plasma, we sent him on his merry way to the beach. As he left us, he was heard to remark, "they'll never get the other one."

Major Stephenson our executive officer decided to transfer our aid station to the confines of the block house, and out of the hot sun.

The heat was terrific that day and the move was a wise one. I reckoned that one of every two casualties that day were the victim of sunstroke.

Thank God that we had plenty of saline which seemed to work wonders in restoring these men who had succumbed to the rays of the sun. (Intelligence had previously reported to us that it rained almost continually on the island and there were only a few clear days out of the whole year.) What a laugh!

About his time, Lovitz was quite ill and rather irrational. I thought it best to evacuate him and did so. Up until then, his job was well done. A report that was later proven false came over the radio at this point stating that Germany had surrendered as if we cared.

My gang was performing magnificently,
breking[sic] into plasma and setting up these
units with amazing rapidity and Dr. Hagerty
and I were running around like mad sticking
them in to the veins of men who needed this
life saving fluid.

Our evacuation system was still going
smoothly by virtue of the amphtracts [sic] and
ambulances and our own jeep ambulance
arrived this day to help in the capacity. As
dusk approached, we were still going strong,
the number of wounded and sunstroke cases
had been terrific to this date.

The galley crew had prepared a hot meal, our
first since we had left the Warren. We ate
like wolves and drank the good hot"Joe"
greedily. There was ample for everyone even
to the extent of two or three cupfuls [sic].

I settled down to sleep on a stretcher inside the blockhouse but had to get up five or six times during the night to treat the casualties. "Mike" our ambulance driver made two trips to the beach that night without aid of lights and over unfamiliar roads.

The next day was to be a duplicate of this one although at the time I couldn't see how it could be possible We [sic] were certainly not winning the battle at least in my books.

The Block House
"Doc" Winer can be seen sleeping in
the foreground (right).

Courtesy: United States National Archives

Chapter 6

Day 4-September 18, 1944

The 2nd Battalion sick bay came up to help us that morning. They were positively useless, helpless and all they did was sit on their dead keesters [sic] watching us work our fool heads off and eating and smoking as they watched. We were running low on supplies and I kept asking them from all possible sources and they soon came rolling in from all directions. Some hot chow came in in off the warren, but we sent it up to the lines, they needed it more than we did.

We couldn't get much news on the progress up front, but we judged things weren't going to well up there at this stage of the game. Charlie company [sic] was taking a terrific shellacking as was Baker company I had no word on my company corpsman and as the day wore on I felt no little concern for their well-being.

General Rupertus, commanding general and General Geiger of the Army drove up to the blockhouse that afternoon. Gen. Rupertus offered a wounded man a cold can of beer, (A magnanimous gesture if I've ever seen one) Dr, Hagerty let him know in noi uncertain terms that relief was necessary, apparently the outburst took the General by surprise for he later told the Med officer in Comm the D. Hagerty was crackin' [sic] up. He was like hell. He was an inspiration to all of us who were with him. He worked like a machine. He directed the corpsman with excellent and rare judgement [sic] pausing in his work now and then to joke with the boys and his running from wounded man to another lending words of encouragement to these boys was an inspiration to all who observed him (Crackin' up indeed).

General William Rupertus (top) and
General Roy S. Geiger (bottom)

Courtesy: Department of Defense (USMC) photo
69010 Courtesy of USMC History Division

On the front lines the situation at this stage was rather critical. Able company had been hit hard from the very first day in an all out effort to hold the lines that formed the beachhead on our left flank. We knew that by their efforts and great fight they had saved us all from certain annihilation as had G co on the right flank that night.

Both had stopped Jap Banzai attacks time and time again that first night. "B" and "C" company's [sic] were on the front lines at the base of a ridge which was to cause the most trouble in the operation. They had been there since early on the 17th. They were exposed almost continually to enemy mortar, artillery and automatic weapons fire. They were catching plenty of hell and every inch of ground gained here was at a terrific cost.

"Bloody Nose Ridge" is what Admiral Nimitz called it. And it was just that. We had previously termed it suicide hill. This ridge was a natural defenxe [sic] area and the Nips took advantage of this fact to the utmost.

From this vantage point they overlooked the whole tip of the island including the airport and though we had taken the air strip, it was useless as long as the enemy controlled the ridge. The nips had mounted a naval 8 inch field gun here and in addition to this, they had machine guns, mortars and artillery all over the place. They were dug in caves and any movement below could be plainly seen. "C" company attacked this installation and succeeded in taking this ridge, but didn't have enough left to hold it as they were low on weapons, ammunition and men, and they were forced to withdraw to set up a line for the night. Things were tough as the morning of the eighteenth dawned.

Chapter 7

Days 5, 6 & 7-September 19-21, 1944

The night's sleep was fair. It was hot and stuffy in the blockhouse and I was aroused several times to treat the wounded. We managed to get these men to the beach although God only knows what they could do for them there at night. Regiment, with DRs. Reed and Sherman came up to the blockhouse this morning. They had supplies and some chow and fruit juice which sure helped plenty. Reg't [sic] dug right in and helped. Good on Regiment.

Dan Krupinski HA1c was killed this morning, like the other corpsman who had preceded him, he died performing his duty this time it was running to aid 1st Sgt. Leukowski of HQ Co a personal friend of mine who also died after he had been placed aboard ship. It gives one a weird feeling to hear that his friens [sic] have gone to their maker. Again, today the casualties were rolling in, but with regiment here to help we handled them easily and with the grace of professionalism which we now were.

Corpsmen MCGill, Thornburg, Napier and Sondler all were working like beavers up there on the front lines with their respective companies we learned and it was gratifying indeed to know that they were doing such a splendid job.

Time and time again we heard that they in particular had run out to treat wounded marines often under heavy enemy fire and at great personal risk, showing complete disregard for their own personal safety. (Their services will be properly recog nized [sic] of that I'm confident).

The day was hot and I decided that' I'd sleep outside that night. Dr. Hagerty and I as dusk approached erected a crude shelter of panchos [sic] and set our stretchers down for the night. We had hot chow again this evening and it made a terrific hit with us all and especially with "C" and "B" companies who had come down from the lines for a spell (I can't recall who had relieved them temporarily).

It was a darn good thing we did sleep outside that night, for a Nip sneaked into the blockhouse during the night and dropped in a hand genade,[sic] which wounded six men.

They got him with a B.A.R., howerver [sic] but everyone was a bit leery after that incident. (Those Japs certainly have plenty of nerve and are fanatical in their all out effort to kill a marine.

One incident that I shall never forget occurred sometime during the afternoon of the 18th. Chief Clark, a full-blooded Cherokce [sic] Indian from our own "baker" Company and had been wounded in the neck and subsequently had lost a great deal of blood. As I administered Plasma to him, he said, "Say, Doc, what's this stuff you're giving me?"

When I told him he replied rather disgustingly, "After twenty four years, I'm gonna [sic] be a half breed." (it's because of boys like this that we win, such indomitable spirit was observed by me not once, but time and time again

Day 6-September 20, 1944

The morning found us hard at work again, our was a sorrowful task, not the work itself for we were well familiarized with our duties, but it's pretty difficult to get used to seeing men formerly very much alive and happy individuals being brought into us on litters some, battered beyond recognition, but theire [sic] spirit was remarkable.

It had rained heavily during the night and Dr. Hagerty and I got soaked, our shelter wasn't much protection and we resolved that if we were to spend another night here we would nuild [sic] something a little more substantial.

"B" and "C" companies again moved out to the lines this morning. They just don't know what it means to quit. What a pathetic picture they made as they straggled by. At least, they had benefitted by the hot chow and the night's sleep.

Casualties were commencing to roll in. And the morning passed swiftly. Lt. Schall of "C" company came up from the beach that afternoon. After a hasty look around, he approached me and asked if he could do anything to help. I told him to watch a saline I.V. and suggested that he wash the patient down, which he did and even commenced fanning him. He continued to do this with other patients until he was called away to the front lins [sic] (Heat, and sunstroke, Exhaustion, Shock, and War Fatigue, were taking a heavy toll of the men.)

I venture to say that 1 of evry [sic] two patients was a victim of one of the aforementioned maladies.)

About an hour later, Lt. Shall returned, only this time he was on a litter, critically wounded and died. His loss hit me pretty hard, for only an hour before [sic], he was so very much alive and so willing to help. I heard that in the short time he was there he performed his job nobly on "Bloody nose ridge."

I might digress for as moment at this point to write about Pfc Moe Serafian. He had been on duty with an Anti-Aircraft Battalion on Guadalcanal and with a buddy has gone "over the hill" and stowed away on the "Warren" He was found and made a rifleman and was attached to "C" company. 1st Sgt, Ainsworth told me of his deed. "C" co. was at the foot of the ridge I previously described and an open causeway was between their location and the ridge itself. Serafian with B.A.R. in tow ran alone over the causeway and under heavy concentrated enemy fire made his way to a cave.

He lured the Japs out with rocks and blasted them as they came out knocking out the machine gun nest and showing the way for the men below. When he'd run out of ammo, he grabbed another weapon and continued firing 'til it was spent. He nearly got caught by a nip behind a huge roick [sic] who cried, "I kee [sic] you marine." "You should live so long you egg headed bastard said Serafian as he opened up."

Serafian was wounded soon after, but as a result of his example and inspiration to all who observed him, he was recommended for the silverstar [sic] medal. I often wonder what his penalty was for going over the hill.

Today for the first time I took a "whore-bath" (from a helmet) and it felt good to be halfway clean. That evening, the galley again had hot chow and we sat and smoked for a while before turning in.

Day 7-September 21, 1944

It *was now early morning and the regiment
had completely taken over the block house.*

*Casualties weren't heavy this date at least
they weren't flowing in our direction and we
had the first break of the blitz. We spent the
day resting, comparing notes, smoking, etc.
Candy, gum and cigarettes had come in and
fruit juice was in abundance. Some mail also
arrived and though we read it, it hardly made
an impression on us. We spent the whole day
in this manner standing-by. Our Bn. what
was left of it were to move up to the lines
again. The major incorporated the remaining
men in headquarters co to some of the hard hit
platoons in other companies. The twentieth
passed in this manner. There were no further
casualties among the men in the Bn [sic] Aid
station.*

Up 'til now our totals read:

K. I. A.-4, Auerbach, Oldham, Johnson and Krupinski

W. I. A., Evac. Bingham and LePage

Ill, Fatigue, Lovitz and Fletcher

Wounded but to duty, Drouin, myself, Mayes, Beal,

Snow, Haterrer, DeRom, Liginski, Atkin, Dyer

Chapter 8

Days 8, 9, 10 & 11-September 22-25, 1944

Today is the sixth day of the operation. What a picnic this has been. Our casualties had mounted to a point where the Bn. was less then one third its original complement. The remaining men were pretty well spent. We were ordered to move up to a point just behind 03 and it was here at approximately1000 that we established the Aid station, making a clearing on the side of the road.

The 2nd. Bn. "pukes" were still with us although they were still cluttering up space. Guadino, the Bn [sic] clerk and I took a walk to the nearby airstrip. Jap mortars were falling occasionally in the immediate area and the significance of the "Ridge" dawned on me.

It was from this strategic vantage point that the "Nips" commanded a view of the strip, and could lob all types of mortar and artillery fire here thus preventing any work on the strip and delaying the landing of our planes.

"Pasquale" and I took a walk around the airfield and stripped some aluminum from one of the wrecked zeros there.

I returned to the B. A. S. where the boys were busily setting things up. We had chosen a spot off the side of the road directly behind a sharp rise in ground level. We dared not pitch a flag, however for fear that it would be seen by the "J" observers.

We no sooner set up when the casualties commenced to roll in. They streamed in at a steady paceall [sic] morning long, though there weren't a great many of them. Most of them were usually serious and three men died on their litters, due to the seriousness of their wounds, loss of blood and shock.

The next group of casualties that arrived were our own stretcher bearer, mess men etc. They had been pressed into service. I thought they were in reserve, but the men told me that they were on the front lines.

A friend, P1 Sgt. Brooks was another casualty; he was hit by a sniper's bullet while chasing (of all things) a chicken. It was at this point when men came running into the aid station crying that there had been two men hit and were lying up in the hills to our left. They had been victims of sniper fire which came from a cave.

"There was a road that passed the blockhouse and hit the road from the airport. That was a pick up point for the wounded, before we put up our tent hospital. Later on they put MPs there to stop souvenir hunters, but they would slip around the guards and get up in the cave area and get killed or wounded. We took turns being litter bearers and then [the Japanese] would get some more shots in. I dreaded it.

One day we got two [souvenir hunters] that was shot up real bad and we fixed them up. I heard one of them tell the other one he was sorry he talked him in to going.

The other reached his hand down for a shake and said he wouldn't have missed it for nothing."[10]

I later learned that these men were souvenir hunters and had no business up there at all. Marsino volunteered to go up with me as he had on three previous occasions. The kid sure has what it takes. He grabbed a "tommy" gun and I my .45 and we took off with our pockets full of battle dressings, morphine, tourniquet and sulfa powder.

Souvenir Hunters

USMC History Division

We ran for perhaps 50 yards up the hill when suddenly bullets started to fly. We ducked but fast behind a nearby concrete station that was approximately two feet wide and three feet high and I'll bet a thread of our clothes wasn't even visible.

We couldn't see the sniper, but we could ee [sic] the wounded men up ahead perhaps 25 yards. I asked some marines who were nearby to cover me while I ran up to the wounded men. One of them was hemorrhaging badly from an artery in his leg and I quickly applied a tourniquet.

I then half carried and dragged him to a semi-sheltered spot and proceeded with the aid of Marsino to patch him up. Stretcher bearers came up and I sent a marine ahead to the aid station with word to have a plasma unit ready.

The other wounded man had not been hit seriously and was able to walk unassisted to the aid station. He was suffering fright and shock more than from the slight wound on his arm. A quarter grain of morphine, a battle dressing and sulfa powder did the trick. (I resolved then and there that I'd never again risk my hide for a souvenir hunter.

I figured that if I were to get it, I'd want to go trying to aid a fighting marine). That morphine works winders in quieting patients down and preventing shock, was very evident to me and another drug I used to good advantage on countless occasions was Phenobarbital which when doled out in doses of 1 grain or a grain and a half was very effective in quieting fellows suffering from "nerves" and jitters.

While digressing, I'd like to mention the great job that was being done by the stretcher bearers particularly the negros [sic] who came up voluntarily from the beach and they worked untiringly. Nothing phased [sic] them. They saved many lives by their daring and constant displays of courage and deserve all the credit in the world,

One of them I recall vividly.

He came down from bloody nose ridge bearing a casualty and I noticed blood on his shirt in the vicinity of his shoulder. I asked him if he was wounded and he replied, "No suh [sic] Doc, I'se [sic] all right, we got to get back up there." He started off, but I caught him cut his shirt away against his protests and found a hole in his shoulder where a bullet had penetrated through completely. Here again is an example of true courage.

"When the 1st Marine Division, on 15 September 1944, attacked the heavily defended island of Peleliu in the Palau group, the 16th Field Depot supported the assault troops.

The 16th Field Depot included two African-American units, the 11th Marine Depot Company and the 7th Marine Ammunition Company. Performing duties similar to their peers in Europe and the famed "Red Ball Express" that supplied George Patton's Third Army with material support, The 11th Marine Depot Company and the 7th Marine Ammunition Companies responded beyond the call of duty and paid the price with the highest casualty rate of any company of African-American Marines during the entire war."[10]

Black Marine Stretcher Bearers on Peleliu

Courtesy: United States National Archives

National Archives Photo 127-GW-334-114329

Black Marines pose with amphibious trucks used to bring supplies ashore and transport the wounded for medical treatment to waiting hospital ships offshore.

In contrast to this let me describe another person. A Navy doctor off one of the outlying ships who drove up to our aid station in a jeep. He had apparently been on a personal inspection tour of the rear and now he dared venture up so close I'll never understand.

At any rate I'll never forget the remark the rotten bastard made as he drove off. He said, "I'd like to stop and help, but I'll miss my lunch if I don't get back to the ship immediately." What a snow job he's going to tell.

It was now about two o'clock in the afternoon. Behind us we could observe some men moving uip [sic] the road in a single column. This was the 2nd battalion of the seventh Marines who had been sent up to relieve our spent and war weary men. Soon after, the remnants of what had formally been our once gallant Baker company [sic] came down the road 24 strong. Some of them were weaving unsteadily from the saki bottle they waved in their hands. They were given permission to drink as the seventh came up.

I recognized Lt. Petruzelli and Sr. Corpsman McGill, and Wassenmiller, Somehow they survived.

I later learned that of the 47 men on the ridge that morning, these twenty four men was [sic] all that remained after charging the ridge. Twenty four men, the last of what had been a company of two hundred and fifty strong.

The 2nd 7th Bn. aid [sic] station had come up to relieve us and we left them as much of our supplies as they needed. We packed up and headed back to the block house. We set up in our old bivouac area for the night and we were all there together, "C" and "A" companies having come down also. We thought we were all done for we couldn't see how they could possibly send us back up there, but we were wrong.

The evening meal was appreciated as usual and it was particularly good this evening, creamed chicken, corn, dehydrated spuds, peanut butter, crackers and "Joe." The night of the 21st passed uneventfully and I slept quite well across from the blockhouse despite the occasional bursts our own 81mm mortars were making as they fired nearby.

Day 9- September 23, 1944

On the morning we received orders to move out again this time to move into reserve for the 2nd Bn 7th the outfit that had relieved us.

The two companies moved out first looking even more pathetic than before. We followed soon after them and went on up the road approximately a mile beyond the point we were the previous day. There were ridges on our right and on these; I could observe ridges that had been battered in the intense fighting that had occurred in these hills. In fact, sporadic firing was still going on here and an occasional wounded man came through our hastily constructed aid station.

Our camping area had previously been a Japanese bivouac area as attested by the storehouse full of rice and signs of a hasty retreat were evident. The remnants of a few wooden shacks, probably living quarter were also visible.

Up on the hill to the right, the firing was becoming more intense and upon inquiring I learned that there were some caves up there had not yet been wiped out and one in particular was causing a great deal of trouble Major Stephenson detailed Lt. Courier to take a squad of up men up there to "clean it out."

I volunteered to go along as the corpsman although Lt. Courier didn't approve of the idea, but I went anyhow. There were about twelve of us including five riflemen, a bazooka team (2) and a flame thrower and two fellows carrying a box of grenades and their carbines. I had a .45 plus my unit #3 (first aid kit).

We carefully made our way up the side of the ridge proceeding cautiously and speaking in either whispers or using hand signals. Only an occasional rifle shot could be heard.

We deployed out in a semi-circle around the objective and being the last man up, I found myself now the closest to the cave. I asked myself, "What the hell am I doing here?"

I saw a rocky shelter about 15 feet ahead of us and as I darted forward for the cover it afforded, several bullets "zinged" over my head and I hit the deck but fast.

It suddenly commenced to rain and it increased in intensity until we were drenching wet then it stopped. The surrounding area was literally covered with dead. The total Jap bodies slightly exceeded those of the marines, but not by many. The positions of some of these dead men were a thing I'll never forget.

They were in all positions and angles. Some glassy eyed some smiling, Looks of surprise were evident on some and on others, I noted they had expressions of contentment and extreme satisfaction.

The Nips all looked the same. Their bodies were a lucrative hunting spot for the souvenir happy guys, I however wasn't interested in any at the time. Later in the day however many of the boys sent off on just such an expedition and some never returned.

Caves turned into pillboxes

Department of Defense Photo (USMC) 107934

As I said, the rain had stopped and we were now whispering our plan of attack. We were to throw as many grenades as possible at the caves entrance to keep the nips back and to give our bazooka men an opportunity to fire at the entrance. We did this with apparent success and the grenades were flying. I even threw a half-dozen or so. (And I'm a non-combatant).

One rifle-man however was wounded in th [sic] head and I stopped to patch him up. It wasn't a serious wound but required a battle dressing and he was sent back. A movie photographer was with us I saw and he caught most of the show.

We all withdrew soon after and the Lt. submitted his report. "Mission successful cave put out of operation plus a certain mention of a combat doctor which didn't displease me.

We spent the rest of the day moping around and setting up shelter in which we could sleep. We were given a hot meal again that evening consisting of Vienna sausage, dehydrated spuds, crackers, coffee and corn fritters a rare delicacy if ever I've seen one.

That night we were attacked viciously by new enemy, mosquitos [sic]. They were everywhere and particularly over me. It was impossible to sleep and I climbed into an enclosed ambulance that was standing by for an emergency.

It was too darned hot in the ambulance so I chose what I thought was the lesser of two evils and went out to combat the mosquitos [sic]. My face, hands and legs were just completely covered with bites as were everyone else who was in the vicinity. In the morning, faces were so badly swollen and eyes were closed on many.

We had to evacuate a few men due to this new scourge. The swelling soon subsided although the itching continued for a week.

Day 10-September 24, 1944

Today we set up our sick bay fly and held sick call. This occupied most of the morning. In the afternoon we loafed around, some swimming others just idly lying around. We had a good supper and settled down once again for the night. It rained cats and dogs at night and my sack was boasting of 2 inches of water. I was forced to get up long before daybreak.

Day 11-September 25, 1944

We learned this morning that we were to be relieved this time for good by a regiment of the 81st Wildcat Division. We were tickled silly at the good news to wait for our doggy comrades in arms.

The Army's 81st Division out of Camp Rucker Alabama under the command of Major General Paul Mueller consisted of about 11,000 men and was assigned to the 1st Marine Division.

By the end of the Pelelui excursion the 81st would lose half as many men killed and wounded then the 1st Division Marines.

At approximately 1500 that afternoon, they came marching up. They looked rather haggard (but then doggies never have the dash of marines) to me however they were angels sent from heaven. Some of the marines made a few unnecessary cracks to wit:" Did you guys bring the U. S. O. with you?" But for the most part, there were few remarks made. Its all yours now doggies.

We left soon afterward via "ducks" amphibious trucks for Beach Purple on the Southern tip of the island where there was no fighting. "A" and "C" companies were forced to hike there however. "B" company no longer existed, its remaining men had been incorporated into "A" and "C" companies and there were only a few communication men, the two Bn clerks and the corpsman left in HQ co.

All the rest were in the line companies. At that, the Bn was a mere shadow of its former self.

We arrived at dusk at Beach Purple. I noticed two LST'S tied up on the crude docks. Their jaws were wide open and supplies were being taken from the ships. We all upon reaching our camp area had one thought in mind, to get into the water. And, this we did. On this beach, the Japs had connecting trenches linked up all the way and I observed several straw dummies they had erected to convey the impression that they were still there.

There had been no landing at this point at all and the Japs upon realizing that there was not going to be one lit out for the attacked beaches.

They left the place in fine shape however, the foliage in contrast to that of Beach white where we had landed was still intact here and was rather a pretty sight. The beach was clean and sandy and we settled down for the night. Soon after, a call came from the direction of the galley "Chow" and we received another hot meal. The galley crew were hitting for 1000.

That night we smoked without the danger of being shot.

Chapter 9

Day 12, 13, 14 & 15-Septemebr 25-29, 1944

Today we learned that we were to move to a nearby island where we were to garrison it. By mid afternoon all hands had moved out except for a few who were left behind with some gear that had to be transported.

Dyer and I stayed behind. We never did manage to get to the other island today and as darkness commenced to fall, we prepared a place to sleep.

There was only one slight incident that marked the day. A ld who was sitting on the beach was struck in the shoulder by a bullet which came from the wooded area inland, we didn't believe that a sniper was there and thought it must have been a misdirected shot, a stray. Bullets will travel four miles. We sent out a patrol to investigate anyway, but they reported nothing.

Day 13, September 26 , 1944

This morning we aboard an amphtrack [sic] heading north by water to the adjoining island where our battalion had gone on the 25th.

Out in the harbor I could see the huge ships and one in particular caught my eye it was a hospital ship lying there resplendent in her green and white covering red cross distinct on her hull and she provided a startling contrast to the drab and somewhat camouflaged vessels that surrounded her.

Our camp area could now be seen from the distance and looked pretty good. It proved to be a fairly good bivouac area. I set up my jungle hammock and in the afternoon we all worked setting up the sick bay. "A" company and "C" company had been assigned the task of preventing the enemy from entering or leaving the island of Pelelieu [sic] which was just to the south of us.

They set up their lines at the northern end of this small island about a mile from us.

I heard from some of their men that they had a picnic, for they were mowing down the Japs who made several attempts to land help to those that were now hopelessly trapped on Pelelieu[sic]. The japs attempted to come in on barges and the marines were picking them off. The amphtracts [sic] would then go into attack and the whole thing was a massacre the nips didn't have a chance. When he boys ran out of ammo, the ruts on the tractor served to chop them up.

Day 14 &15-September 29-30, 1944

We stayed on this island until September 29th. The three intervening days were spent resting and loafing and bore no significant or anything interesting enough to mention. We bathed and picked shell, wrote letter and ate two meals daily. The corpsman held sick-call. The rest did us a world of good and today, the 29th, we learned that we were going back to Pavuvu [sic] on the Tryon a hospital Evacuation Ship.

You can imagine how overjoyed we were at the good news It [sic] was late in the afternoon as we made our way to a large LST. We had been delayed somewhat by the army who had to relieve us before we could go. It was dark as we boarded the Coast Guard Vessel which was to transfer us to the Tryon.

The sea was too rough to effect [sic] a transfer that night so we were forced to spend the night on the LST. It was crowded, the sea was rough as hell and the night dragged slowly.

Sleep was impossible due to the crowded conditions, but at day break we commenced to transfer to the nearby Tryon. Here, we were fed and given our compartments. The chow was excellent and continued to be all during the trip. Today was Sunday, October 1st and Church Services were held on shipboard. We were quite happy aboard ship, but we were anxious to get back to our home in America.

Hospital Ship Tryon

Courtesy San Francisco Maritime Historic Park

Chapter 10

What a waste it turned out to be?   The battle for Peleliu lasted almost three months. Not the four days that was predicted by the 1st Marine Division Commander, William Rupertus. During this brutal contest, both sides suffered devastating casualties on the field of battle.

Officially and originally called "Operation Stalemate," it was the forbearer of two future confrontations that would test the mettle of the marines in more ways than one. What lay ahead for our devil-dogs were the landings on Iwo Jima in February of 1945 and the assault of the Japanese home-island of Okinawa in April of 1945?

In hindsight Pelelui was a mistake that should have never happened. The goal of the 1st Marines and 81st Division was to capture the island's small air strip that would be used to allow American aircraft the ability to hit the Japanese homeland and that was accomplished.

While the objective of capturing the airfield was achieved, the island was never used for its intended purpose; a staging area and stepping stone toward Japan.

After the victory and occupation very few military planes ever landed or took off from Peleliu when the triumphant marines pulled out.

In the historic sense, the entire battle was overlooked and ignored by the Press. All the attention at the time was directed toward General Douglas MacArthur and his heralded return to the Philippines. Pelelui was destined to be a diversion that turned into a slaughterhouse for both sides.

MacArthur received the glory he desired while the marines and the army got the shaft.

"The Secretary of the Navy James V. Forrestal awarded the Presidential Unit Citation to the 1st Marine Division, and its reinforcing organizations, for "extraordinary heroism in action against enemy Japanese forces at Peleliu from September 15 to 29, 1944."

Sixty-nine participants in the battle for Peleliu were decorated with the Navy Cross. The Cross was the second senior-most combat award in the naval services.

On an individual basis, the nation's highest award, the Medal of Honor was presented to eight Marines for gallantry in the fight for Peleliu; sadly five were decorated posthumously, as indicated by (*):

*Lewis K. Bausell, USMC, 1/5;

Private First Class Arthur J. Jackson, USMC, 3/7;

*Private First Class Richard E. Kraus, USMCR, 8th Amphibian Tractor Battalion;

*Private First Class John D. New, USMC, 2/7;

*Private First Class Wesley Phelps, USMCR, 3/7;

Captain Everett P. Pope, USMC, 1/1;

*Private First Class Charles H. Roan, USMCR, 2/7;
And First Lieutenant Carlton R. Rouh, USMCR, 1/5. [11]

15 DAYS OF HELL

The question of whether the Peleliu operation was necessary remains moot, even today, after some fifty-two years after the September 1944 landing.

The heroism and exemplary conduct of the 1st Marine Division, its Marines and Navy corpsmen, and the soldiers of the 81st Infantry Division on that miserable strength sapping island is written in the record.

There is the enduring question of whether the battle and capture of Peleliu was essential, especially in view of Admiral William F. "Bull" Halsey's recommendation through Admiral Chester Nimitz to the Joint Chiefs of Staff of Generals' George C. Marshal, Hap Arnold and Admirals' William Leahy and Ernest King on 13 September 1944, two days before D-Day, that the landing be cancelled.

By that time, it was too late to call off the men and supplies moving forward. The plan was set in motion with no chance for recall.

Peleliu would be added to the long list of battles in which Marines fought, suffered, died and eventually prevailed.

What did the capture of Peleliu cost? Per the United States Naval Department, marine casualties numbered 6,526. Of this number 1,252 were support troops which included corpsmen and doctors were killed.

The Army's 81st Division totaled 3,089 casualties including 404 were KIA (killed in action). Total U.S. troop casualties for the two-week battle were 9,615 for Peleliu, Angaur and Ngesebus, with 1,656 dead.

For most World War II veterans when their service to their country was completed, they came home to parades and fanfare from a grateful nation. America welcomed back its "heroes" with genuine affection and thanks.

For the returning GI's of World War II what lay ahead for most of them were family life and pursuing the American Dream? Other returnees were haunted by what they had witnessed and more so, what they had participated in.

Often referred to as the "Two-thousand mile stare" it was on Peleliu that this condition was first diagnosed. It was best depicted by war correspondent and combat artist Tom Lea.

U.S. Government Public Domain

Per those capable of diagnosing the "stare, a marine suffering was described as one whom... "Left the States 31 months ago. He was wounded in his first campaign. He has had tropical diseases. He half-sleeps at night and gouges Japs out of holes all day. Two-thirds of his company has been killed or wounded. He will return to attack this morning. How much can a human being endure?"[12]

Today we have a term for the disorder that is suffered by some returning veterans. We call it Post-Traumatic Stress Disorder (PTSD). After World War I and II ended it was called Shell-Shock or the "Two-thousand mile stare." Some effects of battle unfortunately never change.

Our Fathers and Grandfathers rarely talked about their time in the military. Most simply acknowledged their service but never went into details.

Jordan "Doc" Winer, when he came back to his home in Salem, Massachusetts. He worked diligently to achieve his goals. Along with his Brother Stanley, they gently helped care for their sightless mother Esther and sick father Barney. They married and had children. Finding time to enroll in podiatry school under the newly-established GI Bill for Jordan it was the stepping stone which would take him to the next stage in his life.

For Jordan Winer, the name "Doc" became a reality as he spent most of his post-war life serving his neighborhood as a Podiatrist in Chelsea, Massachusetts.

Doctor Jordan Winer was remembered as a dedicated husband, father and a supporting member of his Temple and his community. He still found time to make house calls along with weekly visits to residents at the Chelsea Jewish Nursing Home.

At his funeral services held at Temple Emmanuel in Chelsea hundreds of his patients and friends turned out to both honor and mourn him.

What can we say and do about our remaining World War II veterans? "They answered the call to save the world from the two most powerful and ruthless military machines ever assembled. They stopped the instruments of conquest that were in the hands of fascist maniacs.

They faced great odds and they did not protest. They succeeded on every front ... As they now reach the twilight of their adventurous and productive lives, they remain, for the most part, exceptionally modest ... In a deep sense, they didn't think that what they were doing was that special, because everyone else was doing it too."[13]

"Approximately every three minutes a memory of World War II – its sights and sounds, its terrors and triumphs – disappears. Yielding to the inalterable process of aging, the men and women who fought and won the great conflict are now mostly in their 90s. They are dying quickly – at the rate of approximately 555 a day, per US Veterans Administration figures."[14]

Of the 16 million men and women that served, sadly there is only about 1 million left. It is estimated they will be gone in a few more years.

For those of us who served a short twenty years later during the Vietnam conflict it was a different story. Our nation was divided by our excursion into Southeast Asia which many Americans considering it an unjust and trumped up war.

One outspoken anti-war activist, veteran and United States Senator from South Dakota was then presidential candidate George McGovern put it as clear as it could be, ""I'm fed up to the ears with old men dreaming up wars for young men to die in."

I guess some events have never changed.

Just look at our history. Korea, Vietnam, Iraq and Afghanistan: all are examples of old men sending young men off to war. Yes, we may have transitioned from a draft to an all-volunteer professional military, but our military should not be sent solely to achieve a political agenda.

As Henry Kissinger so stated on history repeating itself, "It is not often that nations learn from the past, even rarer that they draw the same conclusions from it."

The Island

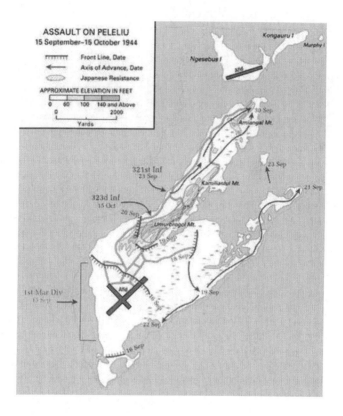

Courtesy: United States Archives

GLOSSARY:

Amphtrac Landing Vehicle Tracked LVT

B.A.R. Browning automatic rifle

B.A.S. Battalion Aid Station

Bn.   Battalion

Chow   Food

Comm. Communications Section

Div.   Division

HA1/c Hospital Apprentice First Class

Higgins Boat LCVP

HQ Co Headquarters Company

Joe   Coffee

K.I.A.   Killed in action

LCVP   Landing Craft Vehicle Personnel

LST   Landing Ship Tank

PHM1/c Pharmacist Mate 1st Class

PHM2/c Pharmacist Mate 2nd Class

PHM3/c Pharmacist Mate 3rd Class

Pl Sgt   Platoon Sergeant

QM   Quartermaster

Rg.   Regiment

W.I.A.   Wounded in Action

Bibliography:

1. Profiles of Known Japanese Holdouts

2. Battle Cry of Freedom 1862 by George Frederick Root

3. Battle of Peleliu, World War II facts January, 2014,

4. Military History Online, Bloody Peleliu, Unavoidable yet unnecessary

5. World War II Campaigns: Peleliu, Museum of the Marine Corps

6. BG Gordon D. Gayle USMC (Ret), 1996 *BLOODY BEACHES: The Marines at Peleliu Page 2

7. Ibid, Page 2

8. Ibid Page 3

9. Matthew Stevenson, Peleliu: A Second Generations Perspective, History Net.com

10. Bernard C. Nalty, THE RIGHT TO FIGHT: African-American Marines in World War II

11. BG Gordon D. Gayle USMC (Ret), 1996 *BLOODY BEACHES: The Marines at Peleliu Page 48

12. Number 438. America's Center Defense Information. Retrieved '06-10-27

13. Tom Brokaw, The Greatest Generation

14. World War II Museum and Veterans Administration

If you would like to see Jordan Winer's personal
diary and accompanying "film clips" from the
actual Fox Movietone News Reel, I encourage
you to visit The National World War II Museum
located in New Orleans, Louisiana.
Their address is:
945 Magazine Street
New Orleans, LA 70130,
Phone: (504) 528-1944 - Fax: (504) 527-6088
EMAIL: info@nationalww2museum.org |
Accession No. 2010.184

NOTES:

53328812R00075

Made in the USA
Middletown, DE
28 November 2017